My Hearts brain and my Minds wicked thoughts

Leeda Fitzpatrick

BookLeaf Publishing

India | USA | UK

Presentation by *BookLeaf Publishing*

Web: www.bookleafpub.com

E-mail: info@bookleafpub.com

ISBN: 9789358316049

First edition 2023

to the scars life has given me.

To my sons—Chester E Ward III AND Elijah A Ward—thank you for believing in your mommy!

ACKNOWLEDGEMENT

I am grateful for BookLeaf Publishing and jotform.com; thank you for the opportunity that allowed me to face one of my biggest fears, leading to one of my biggest accomplishments. I want to thank myself for jumping with my heart first. I want to thank my lord and savior Jesus Christ.

PREFACE

With this book, I hope that the reader gains an understanding of how beautiful they truly are. As I expose the beauty in my beast. I hope the reader finds theirs. No one gets out of life without a scar to prove they have lived it. May you be able to trace my scars in my words and heal yours.

Side-by-side

Regrets and demons "lie" down side by side. They cry, but never out loud. Mirroring every scream. Never a shout. Five hundred and fifty-five thousand miles on Fears Road. Still nowhere to go. The heart yells turn back around. How far is too far gone? When the body leaves yet, the heart never moves on. How big is pride when guilt gives the ride? When forgiveness has run away with your peace? Regrets and demons lay down side-by-side, put them to rest and then you'll see.

Judging

Dear judgmental eyes,
So quickly you speak with just one look.
Loud.
Aggressively.
The way they roll you'd think one could die
from my sight in their eyes.
Your words of judgment are even quicker.
Jack was the reason Jill went tumbling after. Hit
the road, One Looker!
As if blood doesn't run in our veins the same.
As if the heart isn't what pumps it through us all.
Do you not bleed red as I do?
Live while blood still runs through

Tongue of fire

Dear Angry tongue,
So abruptly you arrived today.
Simmering like drops of oil in a frying pan.
Words have the want to fly as if I've added catfish.
Causing pain, shock, may be a few scars left for remembering.
Skin feeling hot to the touch you try to extract my ill words like tea bags,
so I choose to sip slowly.
Swallowing every word, as you cool. I refuse to lose control… shhhhhhhhhhhhhh.
Let every man be swift to hear, slow to speak and slow to wrath.

A longing heart

My King.
Your love reminds me of chai tea placed on the heat at the end of a long winter day.
Just for me, calling for me to squeeze the lemons life has handed me.
You seem to blend so beautifully.
Honey laced. I cradle every sip before it warms my soul completely.
Slowly, sipping with thoughts of us that never end like the love you continue to give me.

Goodbye

My love, mad bulls couldn't pull me away from loving you.
Imbedded in you like a tattoo.
Love tells me what's next to do.
Foolish girl for you.
Now look what you do.
Finally pushed me away from you.
So hard I couldn't stay with you.
No choice other than to fall out of the ways of you.
Falling out of love with you.
Reaching, but never touching you. Again.
I frantically try to love you whole again. In less time than I needed, maybe I'm the reason. Thinking
before I shatter into a billion pieces. I scream goodbye and hope you feel that I mean it.

My

My mind, heavier than gold. How deep are you willing to go to find me? Years run by me. yet you seem to spot me. My soul shines like diamonds in the sunlight. You must have a particular eye to have noticed me. Beyond broken, shattered, and blowing in the wind. The summertime can never be hotter than the attitude I hold inside. I apologize I wasn't born rude. I promise you, I'm made of sugar and spices all that you'll knead in life. Blended never mixed. Hoping that you make it to me before I rise then disappear. Like the smile I once had. Your presence makes me want it back. My heart won't let me do that. It's been beaten, blue-black. Indigo is jealous of that. I probably owe some dough for the dark nights I barrow. My subconscious continues to let me know, it's restless. Only my god can truly fix it. Put me back together again. Just to break the mirror that knows my name. Running down Drury Lane. Dropped more than my gumdrop button. Maybe you will notice that I am the woman for you. My heart, heavier than gold. How deep are you willing to go?

Spelled

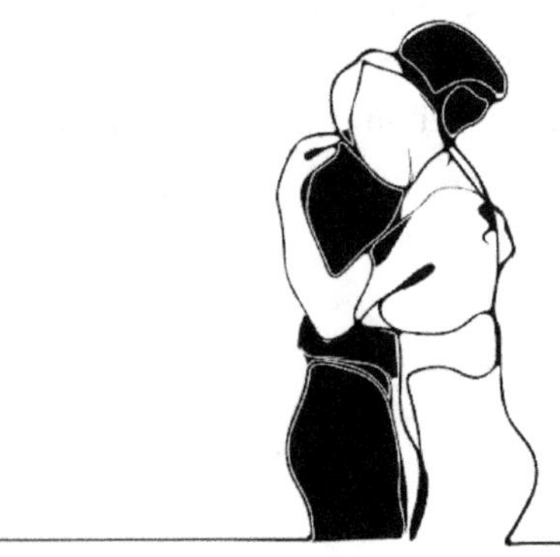

Love. For something spelled so simple, look how difficult we make it. Some of us go lifetimes, unfathomable distances just to fucking fake it. Forsaking it. Huh! Yet craving it. Fresh out of the womb. Love. For it to be spelled so simple you would think that all humankind would know what to do. Daydreams and nightmares, love affairs with movie screens, TVs, and iPhone 15. All of this got damned technology and still no understanding of L.O.V.E within. Love. I admit, how difficult it is to get out. Lock myself into an insane asylum before my lips part like the Red Sea to pronounce L.O.V.E. Love, as simple as 1, 2, 3 look at silly me. Oopsie, the problem? It's me, 24 hours of love songs play in my heart in 3-D

that you might not see and this you won't
believe. I am afraid of love, but it's not what you
think. Not because it hurts so much it's because I
don't care how much it does. Hold on to me! I'm
in L.O.V.E.

Your

Your smile brings light to many lives. Your laughter is the music to many ears. Your gaze puts out flames, sins, and insecurities away, sends chills down the spine of the cold-hearted, shattering every inch of ice. Your walk, gentle, but shows so much strength. Every frown you rejected, flipped it and now you smile because you accept that every up comes with a down. Every ill word you trapped with your tongue. Every fall you've overcome. Every tear you've cried hides behind the glow in your eyes. Every "it will be OK" turned out to be alright. I know why your smile brings so much light. No darkness in sight. It's your right after winning your life battles.

Crowned king

My King, the world has beat you up and spit you out time and time again. I'd say it's because you're so strong, one hell of a man. I might be wrong. Don't be offended. Impressed by how you continue with your strong spirit. Not sure if you want to, but you must hear it. You arrive to me so kind and sweet, full of courage, on bending knee, back straight, head high, silently our eyes meet; where you and I create our fantasies, dreams, and destiny's come true. It's you, you're beautiful, our world sitting on your shoulders. You love me so good I'm sure that I could help you hold it, mold it. Never fold if tomorrow only gave me you. Full of peace. You and me. Yes, I'd quickly choose. Come here to me. My everything. A Crown I'd love to give you. I thank God I have you. More than glad to make a house our home for you. I Crown you as King.

When

When your light starts dimming. When your world stops spinning, while your heart is breaking, hold on, better days are coming.

When "one day" comes

A world full of people. Not sure if you want them to see you. Seeming like no one does anyway. When you shine so bright, the world says not just right. Don't know if you truly want to be you.now a days, such a haze Here comes the "What's wrong?" The "What happened?" and "Why not mes?" along with the "Is it me or the world?" Why can't I trust anybody? Don't want to look like another. To many cookie cutters boys, girls and others, not to forget whatever's in between. A world full of people. Not sure if you want them to see you. Seeming like no one does anyway. If only it was a place to nip and tuck all your baggage so no one can see all of your mistakes. Hide your identity until someone says you're the shit, their honey dip, makes you fit so snuggly. Fraudulence is the next big thing. I'm sure the blame is on this world. One day you'll be someone's everything. Broken spirit, big successes, insecurities included. One day you'll be someone's everything—crooked smile, laughing out loud, healed heart with scars showing bravely. One day you'll be someone's everything. Self-doubt muted. A world full of people. Not sure if you want them to see you. Seeming like not one does anyway. Never looking at the world, wondering if they notice you. One day you'll be someone's everything, all they need and more, all of your pain, all of your joy, all of you— broken down and built back up. Never giving up on you. One day you'll be someone's everything just because you are you. A world full of people. Not sure if you want them to see you. Seeming like no one does anyway.

Loud

Never saw it coming. I guess I just wasn't looking. Jumped into this love pool headfirst, now both feet in. Even started back swimming. You double dog dared me, encouraged me to jump in, now that I'm here, where are you? Screaming out Marco no polo to be found. The old me would've screamed to get out by now. The new me chooses to drown. All of these emotions I just can't get them up and out of me. Heavy hearted, Sinking in a dam full of my tears, confirmed fears, ears opened shut with your "I'll always be here." Why does a broken heart hurt so loudly, but bleeds so silently through the tears I hide? Eyes wide closed, guess that's why I've never seen this coming. Hands tightly closed on our false reality. Maybe I am crazy by now. Heart wants to scream and shout, toss and turn like this undercurrent. I guess I just sink, waiting to drown. Floating anywhere, everywhere and across my boundaries, you gave nothing and I want something other than these broken promises, echoing in my consciousness. Asking myself is this really it? Look what you've done to me! Why do broken hearts hurt so loudly, but bleed so silently through the tears, I cry—Will this be the last blue sky I ever see? Will I ever find the beauty in you letting go of me. "Your everything, your baby girl, your ride and die, your you and me." Silenced my intuition for you and me. I can't believe me. The way you have me second-guessing me. Not sure if our love is dying or slowly growing. If you're surprising me or hiding from me. Silly, silly, silly fucking me to believe you'd catch me. I cry so hard now I can't breathe, so long I can't feel me. Just answer me why do broken hearts hurt so loudly but bleed so silently through the tears I hide?

Shooting star

My heart said, "look up." There you were, standing, looking into my soul. A moth towards the flame. Like the stars in the darkest of night skies, you glow. "My favorite dream." Sweetheart, yes you are, the shooting star. Captivating, amazing, fascinating, taking my breath away. Turning on the good in my bad day. I don't even know your name. My heart hears every word you don't say .This must be our lucky day. I never knew the rainbow wasn't needed for a pot of gold . Oh, boy, you should know. This is the perfect timing, you and I aligning. Please let this moment grow. I watch you fall for me. In my arms you land precisely uniting in the love we both need. Wishing for the same things. Spirit says, run away with me, but

still, we stand. Mesmerized by your presence
and for those seconds. I forget about the moon.

Chi

Your bold love fixed my broken heart, just for
God to wrap you in his grace then guide you to
his gates. There is where my cracks begin again.

Dear Reader

Dear reader,
You're willing to love.
You're willing to help.
You're willing to enjoy, as well as forgive someone else.
You're willing to sacrifice.
You're willing to commit.
You're willing to cheer on progress, growth and loyalty to someone else.
You're willing to let go of happiness, compromise and fight for someone else but you. You have no time for you. You're willing to fight for their rights.
Speak and never think twice for someone who's right by your side when their time is right.
You're willing to wrong your rights.
You're willing to suffer.

You're willing to find the answer, cross the yellow brick road and give them all they ask for. Stay up all night if it means they'll be alright.
You're willing to stress.
You're willing to forget.
You're willing to look past all those times you couldn't get a helping red cent.
You are willing to wait in the rain to follow the rainbow, go places that they will never go. You're willing to give them your pot of gold, from a journey you took alone. Why aren't you willing to do that for yourself? Like a plant with no soil, this can be bad for its health. You'll provide air to life, but live a short one, wondering why no one ever cared for your roots.

Today

If you continue to bring up your past, you'll forget about today. You'll live there forever. For the rest of your days. How beautiful is or was today? Oh wait, too much past on your brain. Can you remember one great thing about today the same way? No more of your "do you remember the time", "that one day", "once upon a time", and "not long ago" you just can't seem to shake it loose. You must let go. If your past is the hot topic-I'll assume you're letting your presence blow past-away with the wind. Live again. Believe again. dream again. I urge you to stop remembering when I urge you to. You have obviously made it through. Stop your past everywhere with you. When today has been

gifted. You must believe this! You can do it!
rewrite that old chapter, with love and laughter.
Forgive that old you with grace and gratitude.
As much as your past walks around with you,
I'd say it owes you a heavy balance and if time
is money then you are rich honey. That's the
possibility of today.

please

My sweet love, please place your head into my
hands. Mountains are lighter than your thoughts.
Our foreheads resting, telling me everything I
know your words aren't ready to. Looking up
into your eyes silently begging for you to stay by
my side. Not to give up. If only a kiss could heal
us. Before our lips meet, let this bittersweet
heart pray your pain away.

Beautiful

Looking into your eyes makes me wonder how beautiful your soul is. So much love you've brought here to me. So much love you always give to me. There's no Money that could go and buy a love like yours nor another that can bring for me to see a love better than yours. Your overflowing kindness put to life's wicked tests; never thinking twice, to me you always arrive. Your tenderness is like Mother and Child. A father's proud smile. A sister's long hug. A brother's tough love and God's "here I am." There you are compassionate, wise and strong. Those who don't believe in angels, man! They are wrong. You're evidence. You are proof. You're the gift I asked of god. You are the truth. Light came into my life flowing behind you. Take me away from here, this hell I walked into for someone who never wanted to come out of it. I prayed. I got you. You looked and you found me, myself and I believe we are meant to be. Looking into your eyes makes me wonder how beautiful your soul is. I'll start with hello then ask who did you follow here, into this hell, I now know. Hell, hold on. If we choose to move on we can get out of here. Leave them here in the hell they choose to stay in. Just me and you on the move towards better days. You and me uniting in monogamy giving our "everything" to one another. Take our heavens to paradise. You look me in my eyes and tell me my soul is beautiful.

Mon-ning Tea

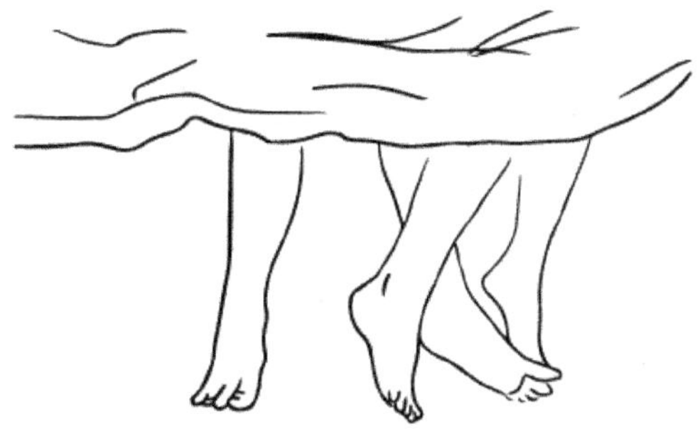

Harder than sugar cubes. Dark chocolate like ground Coffee beans. Soft and brown like the coconut bread we pull in the morning. Fingertips to do the opening. Hotter than the water for our tea, wake me again and again. Sitting on repeat. Lips pressed together as if we'll get another drink. Our taste buds mirroring like waves. Lick you like the drizzle on my glass. Get you off. Swirling to the bottom, watch you rise like a creamer. Mimic the motion of my spoon. Ride the rhythms of my oooh. I love how you do, what you do, the way you do when you do it makes my cup flow over. Our neighbors know when we drink our morning tea from the clink, clank, clinking.

Bang!

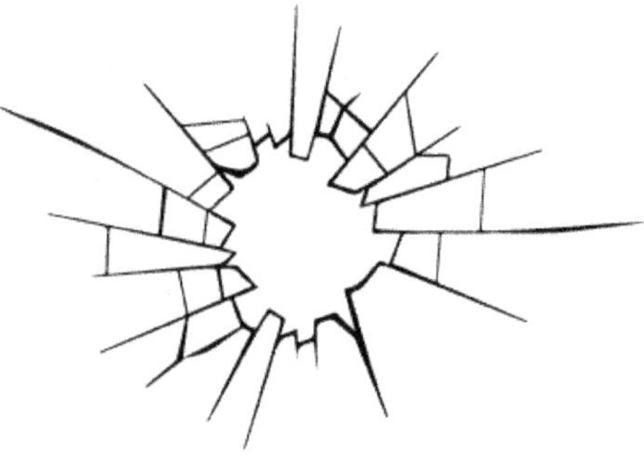

Sniper, no sniping. Bang! What's up with that thang? Puuuww puuuww it's a twenty two. More like a shotgun to the chess. What's next? Heaven sent a sniper. No sniping, give love a rest. I beg. Hands in the air, waving, like I care for you to see me. Your fair warning, smoke falls down the sky. Heat heavy. Strays collected no cat, no dog. Man down next time. Sniper no sniping. Bang! Door off hinges. Smacking bitches I left silently the first time, my warnings are different. Asking for feelings. Now I'm Trippin! Puuwww puuwww. Man down. Call Rihanna, it's twenty-two. Shots taken. Guns ah blazing, Yosemite Sam. Don't get to running na. Feelings everywhere. You're nowhere to be found. Sniper no sniping. Cupid's list checked twice. Got me fighting for my life. Struggling with my last breath. Bang! What's up with that thang? Told I'd be found. Puuuw puuww it's twenty-two. Checkmate. It's too late, your queen has been taken. Slipping and hiding, sliding and lying. Silly rabbit, tricks are for kids, watch your heart disappear. Sniper no sniping. I give!

Under the sycamore tree

Like magnets, we are pulled together with no resistance. Intertwined , our energies mirroring the roots of the Sycamore. Caressed by the sun is warm breeze. Our bodies unveiled. Exposed like the stars at midnight. Tower over me like the shadows of the sycamore tree. Submissive. I Namib. You Welwitschia mirabilis. Grow for me! Our breaths mimic the race of a gazelle running from a lion across the African plains. You've caught me captured in the rapture of your love. I am yours. Vulnerable. Under the spell of your eyes. At the mercy of their depths. I you inch by inch. You receive the depths of my universe. You've invaded my galaxy. I can't take anymore. You're trapped, squeezed between the matter of my walls. You've filled me to the brim, I splash all over you. Rain showers, waterfalls, thunderstorms and cream filled peaches. Melted

chocolate, caramel, and honeydew droplets. I am
dripping for you, the song of my lips, match
your hips. You can hear your name. The twinkle
in your eye disappears like a volcano's violent
eruption. The extreme heat matches my melted
butter cream. Allying our connection.
Destroying everything in its path. Hardened by
my rain storm we create life again under the
sycamore tree.

Sweet thang

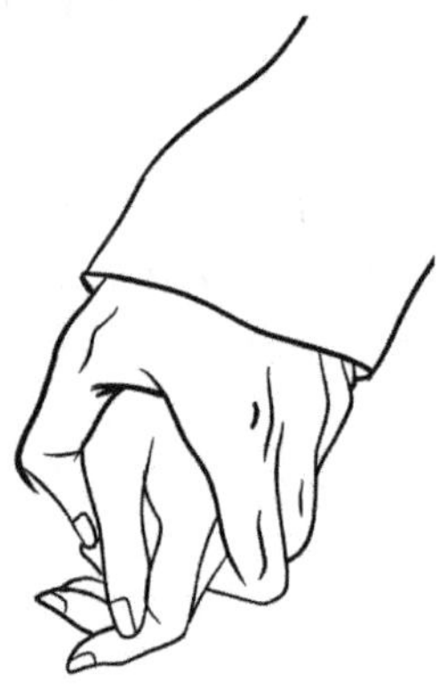

Take my hand and walk me to your heart then let me in. I'm so patient for you no matter how long the walk. The ride. In the fight I'll be by your side, no matter how high the price. Take my gold. My diamonds and pearls. For you are my wealth. If they touch you, it will be a war, a catastrophe. I will lose it without you, so I'll fight like it's the end. You are my life, my lover, my friend. I will fight with every might in me. It's so right. Why do I smile? You. Why have I healed? You. Why do I pain no more? You. I'll fight for you. Just take my hand and walk me to your heart. Don't worry it's safe. You've loved me so good, I'm sure my touch will heal and jumpstart our future. Let our hearts have their way. Locked in a pinky promise let's jump into this love together. Look me in my eyes as we drop into its depths. This deep love, this real love, this soulmate. This, I don't care what my mama or your mama got to say. Walk me to your heart. Let's leave our past so far behind so when we look back it's always been you and I. my baby, my sweet thing, my crowned king. I will love you anyway, here is where you ought to be, with me. Your therapy. Your everything. Walk me to your heart. Let's get lost in the beats of joy they create. Let's be wrong, if it makes us all right, take my hand and never let me go I'll do the same. Walk me to your heart, then let me in.

Ugly cry

I ugly cry when I think of the love we share. I've walked away from so much pain and then you were there. Some days I pray thanking my God for you and all the things you do. My "dream come true." Our reality is so blissful. I ugly cry when I realize the love we share is true.

Dear King

I just want to be good to you. Never go, sweet and slow, always hold onto you. Super glue chokehold. Never let go of you. Soul ties, lint on socks never get me off of you. Honeyed kisses, sugared fingertips, candied corrections and delightful romances. I just want to be good to you.

My friend

You can hide in my love. It's so deep and true.
You can live there until you're ready to trust
again. My friend, you can hide in my love, until
your walls crumble into dust and blow away
with the wind. Until you never build them again.
Until you feel safe again, my friend, you can
hide in my love. It's so deep and true. You can
hide in my love. It's so deep and true and true.

Can you tell

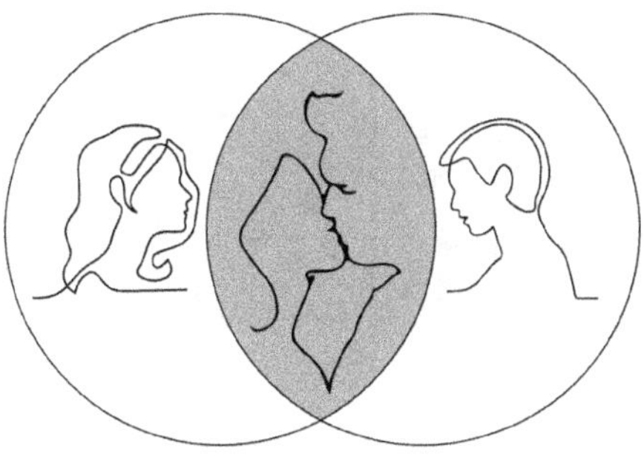

The way you look at me, deprives me of my own sight. The way you look into me you easily expose what I hide. My emotions, my mind. Right down to the soul and spirit of me. It's as if you can see my truths. Truths I've not exposed to anyone. All of me, you read like the Sunday newspaper. I can't hide how much I want you around; nowadays I don't want to either. Looking down so you can no longer see the truth in my eyes. Me falling for you shows through the eyes of me. Can you tell? Can you see? The way you look at me, deprives me of my own sight.

checkmate

Dear King,
I can only imagine whom you thought you were playing with. However, I—your queen—can reassure you that it's not me. Not me at all. Game player! Checker pieces on our chessboard? Get the total fuck out of here. My dear, my protector, your pants are on fire and you're standing in the middle of our kingdom. Now look what you've done! I would call the knights, but you need a Bishop. The way you pawn yourself away like you're not the king. I would have never imagined the one to yell "Off with your head" would be me. Goodbye my captured king.

I can hear your heart

I can hear your heartbeat, it's a rhythm strong like your stance, heavy like the world carry on your back. Maybe that's why my ears pick up the sound of your tears echoing from miles. You still smile. I arrive before your tears hit the ground. Catch your chin before you put it down. Look in your brown eyes and we smile. Our silence says everything be all right.

Until

Take me into your arms until never meets
forever. Until letting go meets eternity. Until you
and I become one heartbeat. Until we laugh,
when they say we look just alike. Until lovebirds
no longer sing. Take me into your arms until
everything means nothing.

Will power

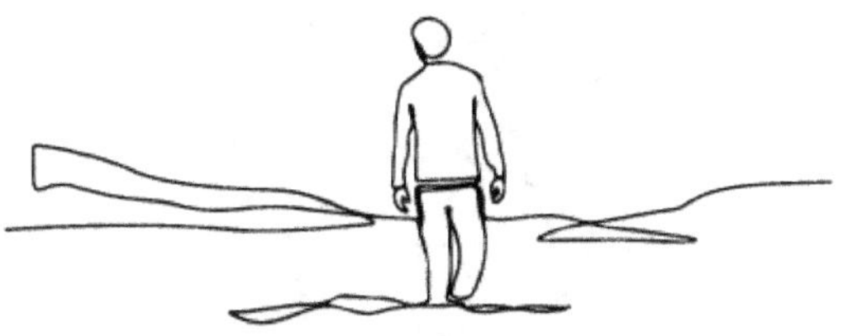

Some days may make you feel like tomorrow isn't worth looking forward to. You've come too far to give up now, believe what I'm telling you. You've gained too much strength. It's not what's on the outside. It's the fight within. For you to just put down your hands at the second you are to win your race You'll make it. You'll make it. Use your will power. Will is power.

Death or everything

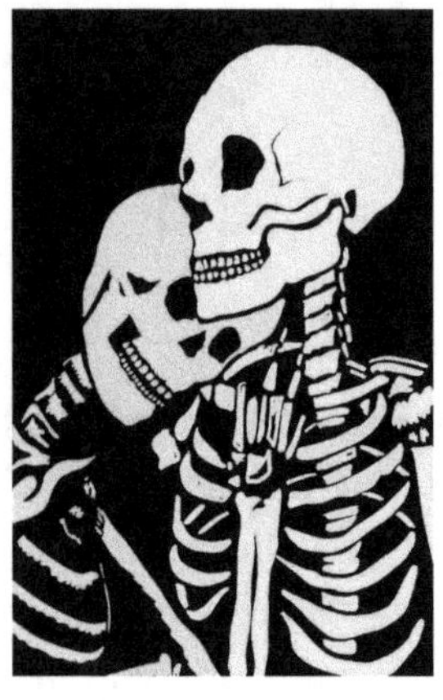

Death. Before we don't ride. Fight until the darkness leaves our eyes. As we pass down our legacy, well worth the sleepless nights. Cheers!! To the release of our fears, but never letting go of our dreams. Death before we do not try, try and then try again. Pull ourselves to the top by our own loose straps, scream and holler when we win. Save every teardrop, our buckets of proof. That, yes, we cried, but we pushed through. Death, before we don't try.

Toxic

It can literally be as easy as and not choose the same old things. This toxic shit, she's a bad bitch. He's a big dick with not one inch to pee, but pissing me off is the way to my heart. Why can't I just get off of this? Merry-go-round with Tweedle-Dee and Tweedle-Dumb and he's with me and she's his queen. It's better if we both just leave separately. I with him and he with me. Let the cash cow run away with the spoon. Just let them both fucking sit in the line of an ego contest, on your mark, get set, let's go. It could literally be as easy as and not choose the same old thing. This toxic shit, she's a bad bitch and he's a big dick with not one inch Pee.

Snakes

Some of us can't identify the snakes that live in our lives, waiting and hiding in the grass-for reasons such as being birthed by them, living, eating or even learning with them. Some of us can't identify the snakes that stand by our sides, because they've been bitten by them their entire lives. Some of us can't identify the snakes looking us in the eye, because that's all we've ever seen. Some of us can't identify the biggest snake that lives deep inside, for a snake can eat a snake, and still survive.

Romance

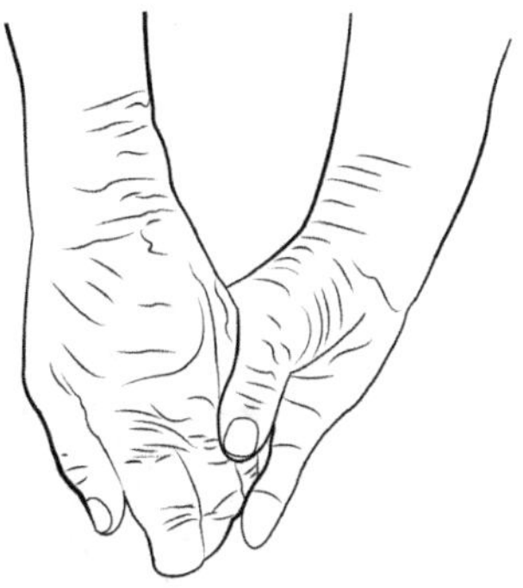

Dear King,

I will love you for a lifetime found in my heart and mind. In the pit of my soul, this I know. I will love you over and over again. I'll fall for you like Pepé Le Pew. We would have a romance of our lifetime, guided by the divine into the realm of you. I'll hold you until you're defenseless. You hold me until I'm vulnerable. May our tears be the water and we grow from pain into joy, crying into laughter, discouraged into encouraged. May our future get the last laugh? I will love you over and over until we get it right. Falling for you like Pepé Le Pew. We could have a love of our lifetime.

Queens cry too

My Queen, your truths could cut gold bricks in two. Your tears could wash nations clean. Your strength could scare any warrior fit for battle. Your power is more than amazing. Your skillful mind is understandable. The depths of your emotions are unfathomable. It's OK to cry. It's OK to question why. It's OK for you not to fully understand. It's OK to stay and it's OK to walk away. It's OK for you not to have words to say. Wipe your tears away when God gives you another day to try in a different way.

The oceans depths

Dear King,
The ocean is a small comparison to the depths of love I have for you, my love, our love can create generations, me, and you, you and I. Try it, take it, taste it. Nothing fake or salty about it. Your queen. My king, the ocean is a small comparison to the depths of love I have for you. You grab my mind, and then my hand as my body follows. Trusting the intellect of you. We grow like the roots of redwood trees. Healing together like the roots of white oaks. Our love can be strong like the ocean waves. Even the ocean is a small comparison to the depths of love I have for you.

Judgment

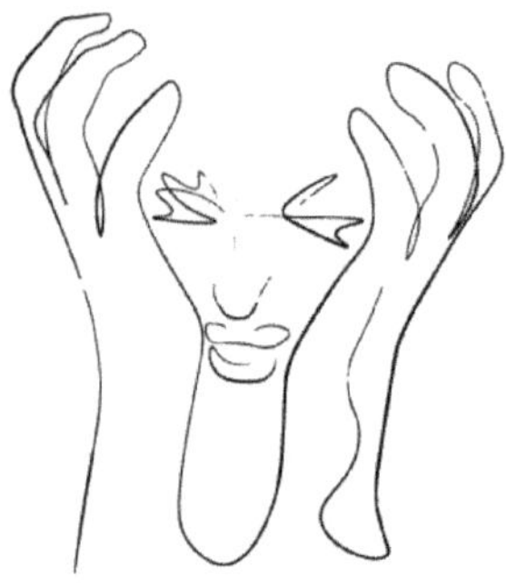

Often, comes around so fast when judgment is at play. How quick does one have to be before they get burned twice for the same mistake? We celebrate judgment. As fast as a lightning strike. No candle for clarity? Riddle me this. Who is the pot? Now identify the kettle. I wonder if both are in the kitchen sink. From the hare to the tortoise, when someone has to admit when they're wrong in their judgment. Seldomly, praising someone for correcting. Changing those old habits. Downward looks and crooked smiles are symptoms of confession, sick! Often, comes around so fast when judgment is at play. When old becomes change, no one has anything to say. When truth is found between lies, who is there to blame? When assumptions meet demise what else will you say? Often we judge so quickly.

Mirror View

How brave you are to face yourself. How wealthy you are to understand the value in your chips and blemishes. How courageous you are in caring for your unique existence. How big of you to step down from your higher placement. How wise of you to not acknowledge all nonsense. How inspiring to believe that yes you can. How sweet of you, being good to you. No negative self-talk. How brave of you to face yourself, all that you are and all that you are not.

Freedom

Trapped in your mind. haunted by your emotions. Triggered by all of your what ifs. Stagnation takes place, freedom and depression, hidden behind a smile. Look around, nothing to hold you down? Drowning from what you hold onto. Go, choose you only. Freedom starts when you get out of your mind.

Seeding

Dear Queen, your strengths have planted many seeds in life, watered by your blood, sweat and tears. May your harvest reach full bloom. May your cup begin to overflow, may your abundance arrive like falling dominos. May you reap every good thing you've dug and sewn. May you be blessed for many years. Your strengths be covered with grace. For you have planted many seeds in life. Watered by your blood, sweat and tears.

God

God knows that you're hurt. God knows that you're tired. God knows when you're lost and confused. God knows when you're just simply being a fool. God knows that there's a strength inside of you. God knows that you're strong in spirit, though you may not feel it. God knows that you will always make it through. God knows life can feel so unfair, like God doesn't care, but God is always there. God knows that the bad will always turn into the good. God knows you can activate the power in you. God knows everything you seek the answers to. God knows one day you'll believe that God loves you.

Mind over matter

Dear King,
Your mind can lead the masses. Your back strengthened from the world's pressures. Mind over matter so you face your battles made of emotions; heart grows ten times. Breaking off the numbness. Yelling, "that's not mine." Your feet have walked many paths, different places, numerous faces, mind over matter seems to get you in spaces of opportunity. How amazing you really are. Mastered your poker face. 911 couldn't take your place, lifesaver, Hero, Angel in disguise, a gift from our creator. All the time you simply get better. Mind over matter, trendsetter, rule breaker, waymaker. Head held high with pride never ego. Your mind can lead the masses. I now understand what they are mad at you for.

Kissed by an angel

Dear Queen,

In silence, you suffer. How loud your pain truly is. Unrecognized by others, you smile to hide the shit. Tremendous is your sacrifice, yet you only know how horrific the things you've overcome. You'll never show it. Kissed by the heavens seeming strong, and independent. An angel. Letting god handle your enemies' pain, betrayal, deceit, don't forget the shame of it. Calling on your God asking for clarity and strength, pleading to be shown the way. Always pray. Change will come now or one day. Then they'll all say I remember when you were different. Funny how you've changed. Your silence is no

longer needed. You sing about your sufferings.
Your joy is louder than your pain. You smell
over and over again. your horrific past has
become your friend, you've flipped it, and turned
it into a bag. Kissed by the heavens, the promise
of Abraham, your abundance allows you to
remain independent and strong. You're an angel
yes, an angel for you pray for your enemies, the
betrayal and deceit to be washed alongside their
hurts and pains. Maybe one day they'll say,
"because of her I changed."

How many

How many times can a heart break? How many times can it heal? Falling out of control, seems to be the only thing that's real! Making cents! Sense, do you have? Out of this deal only pennies are collected. For Love, and all of its what ifs. Give it all up with no gun held high. Casper can see your lies. Blinded by the heavens, shining truths down on me. Silly me to think a heart can break one million times for love's sake? How many times can a heart break? How many times can it heal?
How many times can you trust again before you believe love isn't real?

guilty conscience

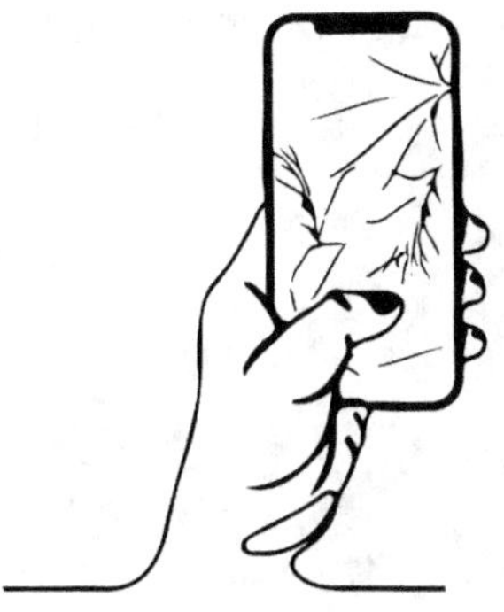

A guilty conscience is what a guilty conscience does. Funny how I'm the one to blame. My truth's drowned by your lies. You see me, doing everything you have. What a shame. Take that! No diddy needed. Shaking off your love for entertaining raggedy bitches. My Ears itching, hoes must be fibbing with their Ol' side-mouthed, bed-backed bitches, but that's your pick of the litter box. Your shit rapidly heading to the left because you don't know right. All night. That dirt flung at midnight, sunlight comes up to expose that a guilty conscience is, what a guilty conscience does.

Homeless Heart

I cut my sleeves off, so that my heart had
nowhere to live. Antarctica would freeze over in
my chest from the thought of you. It used to be
painfully clear. Laugh loud joker! Even Harley
quit. What's love got to do with it? Through
with it. Blew it all into smithereens. Then row
me down a river where life is but a dream of a
single me amazingly happy. Not caring about a
thing, I cut my sleeves off, so you had no access
to me. My heart has nowhere to live and I can
give a shit now that I'm a bitch and it's
obviously clear that I no longer want you here,
near me, around me. Don't bother, I'm good.
Remember when I was wishing you better?
Now, I wish a motherfucker would. I cut my
sleeves off so that my heart had nowhere to live.
Freezer in this bitch. Go get Omarion, don't

touch me for shit. Laugh louder, Woody I hope
your Pecker falls off. Row me down a river, your
ring, where it is tossed. Where life is but a
dream, hear me sing merrily merrily merrily,
stay the fuck away from me.

The end

Pushed to the end of us, broken before I even hit the ground. I fall all over you. I'd guess we've found BooBoo's last name Dafoo. What a leap. Congratulations, it's over! Mend my heart with the knives in my back you put in. It seems like I love pain. Pushed to the end of us. Bounced like broken trust. Begging God to stop the numbness I want to feel this one.

We meet

Eyes to eyes, lips to lips, heart to heart is where we stand. Patience filled with joy, wrapped in our tears, dropped like water cupped in hands. STOP. Breath to breath, soul to soul, energy to energy is where we stand. Love full of our fears, wrapped in the vibrations of our laughter. Today into forever.

Faith

There's a power in faith so hold onto it. There's a strength in Faith so lean into it. There's a blessing in faith, so look into it. There's a healing in faith, so be full of it. There's a freedom in faith so step into it. There is a miracle in faith, so believe in it.

Many enemies

One of the hardest enemies to fight is the enemy within. May you find the key that will set you free. May you find a way to release your pains, the best way you know how. One of the hardest enemies to fight is the enemy inside. Running from your past no one truly knows drinking down your sins, the memories come and go. Smoking out your fears, anxiety controls. One of the hardest enemies to fight is the enemy within. May you find your peace starting within.

Flaws

Flaws are like cakes and pies. Everyone likes something different no matter if it's good for them or if it isn't. Shake that thang or move silly, stand on the wall or get jiggy. Some like them tall, round and/or skinny. Others don't mind if you're bald or mini. Flaws are like cakes and pies. Everyone likes something different no matter if it's good for them or if it isn't. Some like them ambitious, tall and full of riches. Others find their diamonds inside of battlefields or ditches. You can't forget about Kay's jewelers, or that friend shoplifter. Flaws are like cakes and pies. Everyone likes something different no matter if it's good for them or if it isn't. Some like them sweet and spicy, rough around the edges, others like them intelligent and kind may be a gamer, NBA ball player, entrepreneur. Maybe a Walmart supervisor if they're genuine. Flaws are like cakes and pies everyone likes something different no matter if it's good for them or if it isn't.

Never give up.

Dear Queen,

Heavy-hearted, scattered mind, overwhelmed with emotion. Something comes when doing nothing isn't an option. Never give up. Keep going. Good fight, day, and night. Head high, you stayed devoted to your dreams. Duke's up, faith filled, larger than a mustard seed. Never give up. Keep going. Something comes when doing nothing isn't an option. You continued on your path when it seemed like there was no destiny. Chaotic days, short nights your dreams turned into your reality. Something comes when doing nothing isn't an option. Never give up. Keep going. How proud you should be for not giving up.

Good girls

Who wants to be a good girl? Oh, how it hurts. How it hurts so bad. Never making it across those tracks. Smashed into reality. Maybe men do cheat themselves out of something beautiful. Who wants to be a good girl anymore? Oh how it hurts. How it hurts so bad. May the rain never stop. My smile doesn't shine as bright. I'm sure they'll find out. The raindrops are my tears falling from the sky. Who wants to be a good girl anymore? Oh, how it hurts. How it hurts so bad. Never getting across those tracks. When you pick up my pieces please leave my heart behind. Who wants to be a good girl? Oh, how it hurts.

dangerous

Danger has come. I've seen that look before. Through the fire, waterfalls, driest desert and thunderstorms, they've crossed the wire to get a glimpse of my love. Risking it all just to damage the dream you stand in front of. Danger has come. A chance to lose yourself. In a timeless love. Through the bombs and grenades, looking death in the face. I stay. Risking your reality, after everything is faced. Running back to the familiar I wave goodbye! To that look in your eyes. Danger!

Ashes into dust

I've envisioned love so vividly, I almost forgot the reality of its truths. I'll cut myself free with the knives I took out of your back ten times. Investigating fingerprints; counting, three. Yours, mine and your enemy. Your eyes closed, wide, revealing I was pulling the knives out of your back when you looked at me. You shove them through and through my heart that beats for you. Cutting all soul ties, gorgeous lies, and fantasies that lived in my spirit. Our eyes meet. Look at me! Love flashing like horror scenes. How fast can I fall out of love before dropping onto my knees? Ashes into dust my heart hits the ground. I envisioned love so vividly, I almost forgot the reality of its truths. You could at least look at me as you "lie." Me to rest in pieces.

Into love

Falling, falling, falling into love with you, dripping like honeydew. Me better than any other honeysuckle, my love for you makes you better than any other. Falling for you, you are the sun shining from within. You are once again my sweet love, my great friend, my made family, and my honey. My baby, my hubby, my daddy, and my king. My everything, my everywhere, if there's any in between. Falling, falling, falling with no brace for impact. Wanting to feel every moment of this. Bring me pain, I'll find pleasure. Give me love and I'll find forever. Hand me truths I'll find forgiveness. Give me your tears I'll find the strength, falling with you no gap between us. Smiling all the way to

forever. You and me, who knew falling with you
would make me better. Dusting those fears off.
Hold my hand, we will make it there. Falling,
falling, falling in love with you.

All alone

All alone. Alone with me, myself, and I couldn't be happier than that fat kid who got the cake and ice cream. All alone. alone with me, myself and I found out that time slows down when love songs play! Man, do they play. How they play every word you never said out loud. I scream. I scream for you under my breath. Holding onto me, myself, and I find places that remember your touch, your lips, your fingerprints to be bone deep. Alone with me, myself, and I now know how I taste. Your face replaced with mine. Fingertips tracking your trails. Rocking, rocking, exploding like a fire hydrant hit on G street. Me. Who I don't let go. Who never leaves. Who always looks out for me, myself and I found out I can bend, stretch and amaze like butterflies. Oh me. Oh my, fucking self. All alone, alone with me, myself and I found out how a flower can be my best friend. Fighting for the first touch. To the sweet end of me. Gently bruised peaches washed in cream. Oh me, oh my all alone. All alone. Me myself and I.

Be fruitful

Better days. Corrected Ways. Time arrives with karma. Planted seeds and tears used for water. Fruit to pick. Some will fall rotten. Better days. Corrected Ways. Time arrives with karma. Lemonade, iced tea. The apple doesn't fall far from the tree. Seeds planted. time taken for granted. What you sow is what you'll reap.

A man can love.

He loved her deeply.
He loved her strongly.
He loved her passionately.
He loved her to the bone.
He loved her when she cried.
He loved her when she was wrong.
He loved her selflessly.
He loved her and she lied to him.
He loved her when she wouldn't come home.
He loved her when she texted, but wouldn't
answer her phone.
He loved her absence.
He loved her when the boys told him to move
on.

He loved her over and over again when a
different man would show up over again.
He loved her long.
He loved her sweetly.
He loved her patiently, honest and true.
He loved her until his heart was black and blue.
He loved her when she left him, lonely.
He loved her until he met me.

Please stay

My hope is so high it blocks the sun. Don't run, don't run, please stay. I feel so exposed. Your eyes, ultrasound my love, growing, slowly showing everyday. Don't close your eyes. Who needs to blink when love is in their face? One blink and it's gone. Time waits for no one, wanting more one on one time with you. We need to be in sync, while we sit and see through the darkness. Let our hopes be higher than the stars, past the galaxies. Don't run, don't run, please stay. Heaven guided. Colliding into two. Where are you? You find me in your heart. Same place, I find you! Is that mercury? My Saturn! I'm your Venus. Nothing but space in between us. You miss us. Mr. "I don't know" did it. Sitting in oblivion. Hopes so high. From Loving you. They say I'm crazy for trusting you. Well,

maniacs deserve love. Don't live here anymore.
Don't run, don't run, please stay. Hit this. Don't
trip. I'm one hundred percent the shit, you hand
me; I'll hand you back. It's a 'stick up put your
fucking heart in the bag.' Goddamned if I leave
without you. I hate you, but I truly don't. You
find me in your heart. You say I'm your home.
I'm lost. I'm so lost in your realm. So high, so
high, so fucking high I see differently.

Another Letter

Dear King,
Your appearance doesn't resemble your worried night. The faith in your eyes would never expose the tears you've cried… you hide. In vision's plainview. Your smile never breaks to reveal what you are going through. Big risks. Shot high. Bad choices and long regrets. Your mind was blaring, your heart beat was absent in your chest. Pray louder. Harder. Longer with your last breath. How protected you make me feel in the world where I feel abandoned. I am all in. By your side I'll never leave. Pull you close. Hold you tight, our love as iridium. My heart for your meritorious commitment. My all to you. My everything. Protected. I want you to feel safe with me. Home with me. Valued and never taken for granted.

Mother

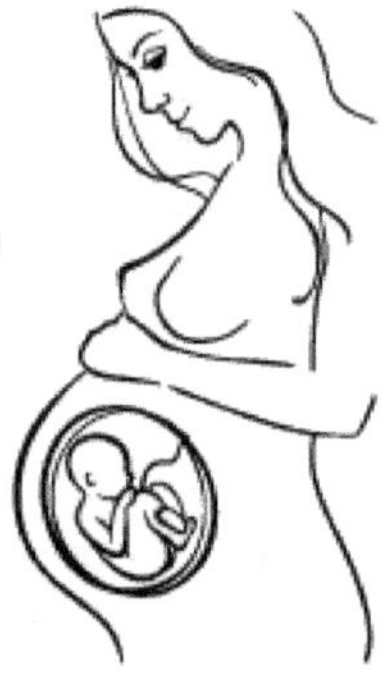

Dear mother,
Where do I start, the healer of all BooBoos, even the ones on the heart. How can I thank you mamma? It just doesn't seem like enough. Thank you for teaching me how to be sweet, kind and tough. Self-sufficient, independent and proud to be who I am. To carry poise, class, and always do the best I can. Thank you mamma for all of your calls and texts, the ones I answered and the ones I didn't. The ones that help correct me. The ones that made me fussy. The ones that pushed me, the ones that calm me down. Thinking one day they'll all be gone, but your love will live deep in my soul. I'll always have your wisdom to lean on. Thank you mamma for forgiving this foolish child. No matter if I was right or wrong. Thank you for never saying, I

told you so, you welcome me with open arms,
To always have someone to run to in times of
pain or joy I'm grateful for that someone is you.
I now understand; at 35, I have nothing figured
out, and the older I get I see in your eyes that life
will work itself out. I can only imagine raising
seven children with my own two hands. Thank
you mamma for holding on like you did, fighting
like you did, never giving up. Always showing
up, making this poor black girl feel like a queen,
stand, omit and correct . I can hear you say it
again and again .Thank you mamma for always
showing us strength on your weak days, the way
how wrongs can be corrected, and how flaws
can be embraced. Thank you mamma for
showing us love when the world was so tough.
Thank you mamma for giving us everything you
had when you had little to give, thank you for
loving us when we didn't get it. A foolish child I
looked around. I now understand mamma, as a
single mother I continue to discover that Choices
and decisions are always for the best reasons
until another year comes around and still I'm
trying to figure things out. Thank you mamma
for your faith when you were down and your
grace when the ups came back around. The older
I get the more I realize that time owes me
nothing, days will continue going and I don't
know much of what's coming or going. Thank

you mamma for your tough love, for your faith and your encouragement for being there for everyone. Thank you mamma for showing me Jesus. Thank you mamma for your prayers and good wishing. Thank you mamma for being my mother, friend and sister. Thank you mamma for being everything I needed. Thank you mamma for believing in me. Thank you mamma for loving the imperfect me.

Time

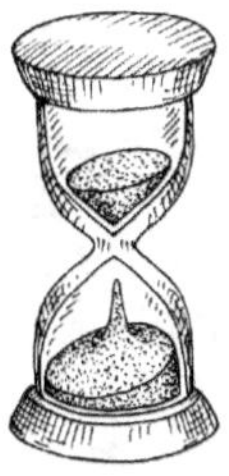

Time. Is it real? Yet we still count, pain has a punch that echoes from inside out, how can we figure it out? No one knows what "it" is. Erasing any doubts. Pushing to the finish line. Destiny is all mine. For the rest of my lifetime. Time. Is it real?

three strikes

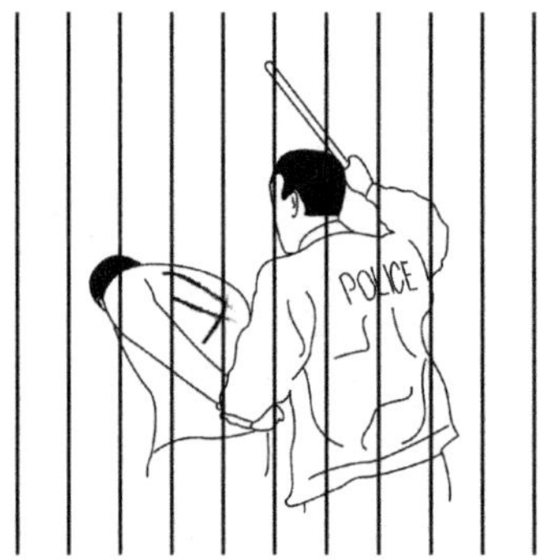

I find it contemplative; knowing that now or later, everyone will need second chances. Maybe even thirty tries to wipe their eyes or sing sweet goodbyes .Reason why a cat has nine lives to get it right. Mistakes, the secret recipe of life's pie, just one slice, but three strikes and you're out. What if someone begs and pleads on their knees? Or change their mind from wicked to good at the last minute? Bad ending. Scary beginnings. Is that it? Three strikes and you're out? Maybe, that's why we have one life. I find it contemplative that some of us take longer to understand the mistakes . Some of us take longer to fix mistakes, some of us take longer to get started again. Some of us take longer to retry again. I find it contemplative; knowing that now or later, everyone will need second chances.

Maybe even thirty tries. Maybe that's why the world turns so we may have three hundred and sixty-five days to make things right. Not three strikes.

Let me

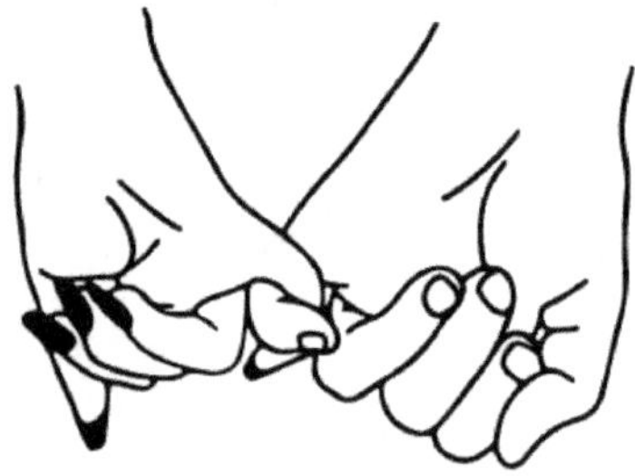

If you let me love you, everything you needed. Everything you wanted. Everything in between. I do mean, all things, anything you ask or need I will do for you. If you let me, I'd trace my taste buds across your skin, bend for you. My strength will never break. Your pretty, kinky, sexy, freaky, little juicy, bad girl on you. So good to you. If you let me love you. I will show you why hard things fit in tight places. Softness makes your power shake. Legs give you your space. Take it. If you let me like you the way you love me things could be so amazing.

Painted faces

Let's face it. You played in it, my face expressionless. Dance clown! Dance! Your sorrow, bigger than your shoes. Jimmy Choo, Balenciaga, your soul deserves "payless" attention to your ego. Bozo, 50 clowns, jumping out of your benz'O! Look at you, Lou!! Keep it up, smack with the melanin inside. High five your pride with the strength of Ike! DANCE like killer ants are in your pants. Show out the same way as if I'm not looking. Let's face it. You played in it. My face that is. Bust a move like a balloon, deflated. That fake smile, disappearing crowd, the circus will end and you'll still choose to be a clown.

New Nevers

Peace has never tasted so good. Never do I need to eat. Love has never felt so warm. In winters my heart sleeps. Joy has never been so consistent. I show all my missing teeth. Never will I ever not smile again. Trust has never been so sweet. Never will I complain about its bitterness. Never will I forget that you're the important ingredient.

Angels in the darkness

Falling into the darkness, I've jumped after you,
I protect my light knowing it'll see us through.
Monsters know my name. Demons too. Bring
my light to any darkness. They thank me too.
What's a beast to an angel? Please tell the truth.
Falling into the darkness. I'm living proof.
Pleading the blood of Jesus over you. Knowing
that it will cover you. You're so far gone.
Physically there's nothing much that I can do.
Wonder why you never hit the ground? I prayed
for you. Falling into your darkness the light will
see you through.

Sinner

They say no way she's a Christian woman, two children, no father, no man would ever want her. Sinner, sinner god ain't in her. How dare she call upon the father. Find her a pirate ship, her Afro-American vernacular is horrible. They say no way she's a Christian woman, all those time she goes out clubbing, no one would want her. As if they weren't of this world, the last time she checked, we all were. So fast to judge her, sinner, sinner God ain't in her, look how she wears her clothes. They say no way she's a Christian woman, as if the woman fully covered, couldn't be promiscuous, what happened to looking deep within, past someone's clothes or skin? As if every pastor has more than the first lady. Like the youth pastor ain't running around playing with these boy babies, how the elders in the pulpit talk about everybody being crazy. Defensive I am if she is me. I'm just saying that

I come to church as her, I am the message she
still receives. Their judgments don't phase her.
How do you say that she doesn't believe the god
that reveals to her. Her unspoken prayers, alone
she'll stand by her faith, she communicates to
the King of all Kings. Her Lord and Savior. She
believes. Jehovah-Jireh, sees all and everything.
Sinner sinner, they say no way she's a Christian
woman. Smoking weed, then on her knees,
praying to be covered with the blood of Jesus.
Mistakes by pound, lessons by dozen, blessed by
kilo, who are they to say she's only a phony. If
God says she's chosen. Only God can judge me.

Ups and downs

Life is full of ups and downs. I guess roller coasters are fine. Some of us scream and shout, the others go silent and numb. Foolishly we run back around and stand in the line. Forgetting what we have already been through, giving life's roller coaster one more try. When you trip on life lessons don't just get up and go. Take a look around and see what you tripped on.

Boys

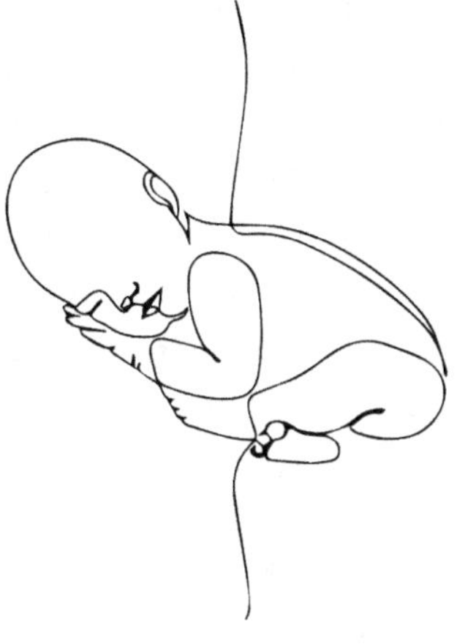

My boys, my strong, wise and powerful boys. I love you more than you know, believe me. It's not easy but I will never give up. Mommy working two jobs. Seems like I'm not doing enough at home. It's a catch 22. Dang if I don't, dang if I do. Work really hard or stay at home with you. Days go by so fast, you've grown in a blink of an eye. I remember when you would wake up and try to open my eyes. Ask me what I'm eating, then put your nose to my mouth. Hold me when I was leaving. Now it seems like you can't wait for me to get up and get out. You would ask me for a helping hand, now you can do it all by yourself. From crying to crawling, walking to running. I remember when a box was the best prize in the world. Now you need more V bucks, a cash app, and cars. Big boys right now, eventually strong men. I wish I had it all, give you everything if I can, but more than materials. I want you to know that you're both kings. Stay honest. Be true and love yourself the best you can. Hold on to one another no matter how bad life gets. The world can get so wicked. So be the goodness in it. Don't let it change you from the good man you can be. Work hard, stay focused and be good to those who are good to you. Everything that glitters like gold is not always good for you. Most of all, know that there's a God that knows you. When times are hard, call Jesus. When words won't come out, pray in your silence. You're handsome, you're funny, you've got all the cool moves. You're athletic, charismatic. Real cool dudes. My boys, my babies, the biggest loves in my life. One day you'll be husbands, treat your wives right. With love and care, time and patience. Fun and stability. Be the best fathers that you can be. My babies, my boys, my sons, you'll always be mommy's number ones. You mean the world to me.

Forgiveness

You have a heart full of pain. A mind full of shame. And a soul full of regrets, that you haven't forgiven, yet. God is waiting for you to make the move towards forgiveness.

Try

Caught in the illusions of life. As reality passes by. Stuck in the past, as another day arrives, captured by the what-ifs of tomorrow, you forget to even try today.

Imposter

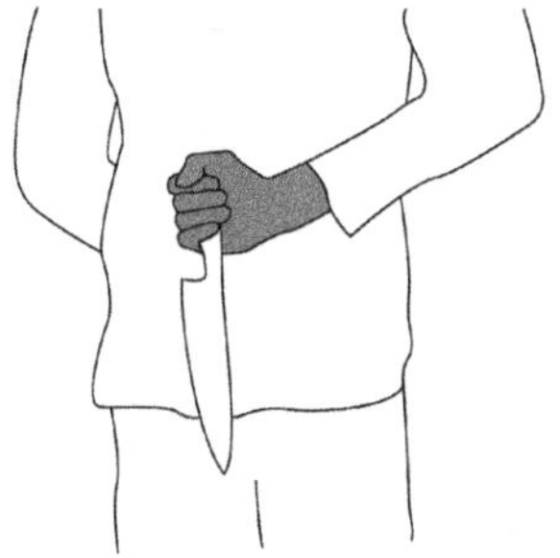

Imposter in your garden. Even the snakes slither away. You continue to forgive, trembling in fear, from a truth that will never kill you, yet you stay and die anyway. Imposter in your garden. You bring them the sun, food and water. The snake won't come into play, yet you stay trembling, from a fear that will never kill you. There's an imposter in your garden. Trying to kill you.

www.ingramcontent.com/pod-product-compliance
Lightning Source LLC
LaVergne TN
LVHW050915200726
843508LV00011B/2203